To: Adams Baby
From: Carolyn Rae

THE
Candymaker's Gift

A Legend of the Candy Cane

by Helen Haidle
Illustrated by David Haidle

Tulsa, Oklahoma

The Candymaker's Gift
ISBN 1-56292-150-9
Copyright © 1996 by David and Helen Haidle
4190 S.W. 195th Ct
Beaverton, Oregon 97007

Published by Honor Books, Inc.
P. O. Box 55388
Tulsa, Oklahoma 74155

Dedication

This book is a testimony of God's faithful care.

To our Sunday School 3rd-6th grade students

who inspired this story by sharing the candy cane's message with others.

To Hannah Boland (our sweet "Katie")

and the other children who posed for the illustrations:

Lacey Boland, Cory and Eric Ellis, Jason Andersen, Drew Shelanski,

Stuart Eagon, James Biggs, Mary Thompson, Kara Wigowsky, and Krissy Allsup.

With special appreciation and thanks to Bruce Craft, David's prayer partner,

who posed as the "Candymaker."

Acknowledgments

Thanks to our "favorite" daughter, Elizabeth Haidle,

for her creative illustrations on the last four pages of text.

Thanks to our Critique Group:

Jeannie Taylor, Barbara Martin, Roseanne Croft, and Stanley Baldwin.

Thanks to fellow writers:

Connie Soth and Elsie Larson, Mary Starr, and Judy Craft.

And thanks to our many friends who prayed for this book.

We love and appreciate all of you.

THE
Candymaker's
Gift

$\mathcal{L}$ong ago on a cold wintry morning, a warm light glowed in the windows of a candy shop. The old candymaker shuffled to the front door and hung an "OPEN" sign in the window. Then he began to prepare for another busy day. He put on his apron and added another log to the fire in the pot-bellied stove. All the while he smiled, thinking about his seven-year-old granddaughter. *What can I give my Katie-girl for Christmas? She's such a joy to me. I'd like to surprise her with a special gift.*

$\mathcal{H}$e reached into the bottom cabinet and pulled out a wooden chest. Unpacking a hand-carved Nativity set, he carefully arranged the painted figures in his store window. The shopkeeper bustled about, cheerfully refilling the candy jars with mints, butterscotch drops, jelly beans, and candy sticks. He chuckled, thinking about Katie and the village children. He knew every child by name — **and** he knew their favorite candies!

*L*ooking over his list of Christmas orders, the old man marked an "x" beside

the names of families with children. *I don't want to forget to slip an extra bag of candy*

into their orders, he thought. *I wish I could see the children's faces light up when they find*

the candy surprise I've sent them.

Humming a Christmas carol, he opened the cupboard and brought out an assortment of

sugars and flavorings, sacks and ribbons. Suddenly, the door bells jingled and a blast of wind

and snow blew into the shop.

*T*o the old man's delight, a group of children scurried in like a flock of little birds. Laughing and talking all at once, the children crowded around the candy counter, their faces glowing. Little Joey pressed his worn mittens against the glass case. *Times are hard since his father died,* thought the candymaker.

The older boys and girls laid their coins on the counter and picked out their favorite treats. The shopkeeper smiled and chatted with them as he packed the candies in small bags and tied them with red ribbon.

"I can't wait until we decorate our tree on..." Ben started, but little Sarah interrupted him. "I can't wait to see the china doll I get for Christmas!"

Two of the girls were silent. *Kara and Marianne know there will only be a few small presents in their stockings,* thought the shopkeeper.

Chung piped up excitedly, "Our school Christmas party is on Friday!"

The old man laughed. "Chung, you always love to have fun!"

"Oh-oh! Time for school!" said Ben, hearing the clock chime. The candymaker quickly passed out the children's sacks. Then he handed a special bag over the counter to Joey. Clutching the sack with glee, his little eyes sparkled.

"Thank you! Merry Christmas!" called the children as they waved goodbye and scrambled out the door. Watching them from the window, the old man looked down at the manger set and remembered seeing his father carve it many years ago.

The children get so excited about the holidays. I hope they won't miss the real Gift of Christmas, he thought. He walked to the back of the shop, knelt by his chair, and prayed, "Dear Lord, You know and love these children more than I do. How can I help them see Your Gift of Christmas? Show me how I can bless Your precious little ones."

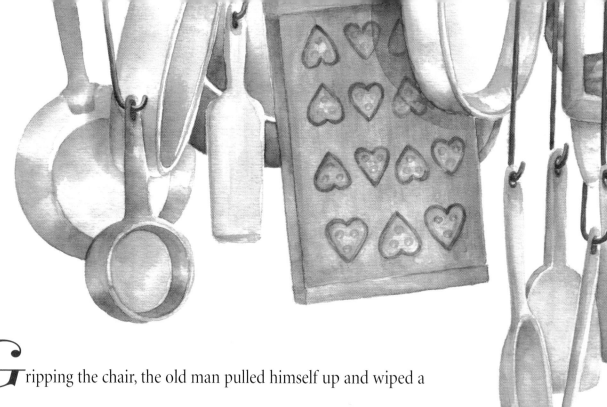

Gripping the chair, the old man pulled himself up and wiped a tear from his eyes. "I need to cook another batch of candy sticks," he said, reaching for a heavy iron kettle. He measured cupfuls of sugar and syrup into the pot and lit the kitchen stove. Patiently, he stirred the candy mixture with a wooden spoon and waited for it to boil. When the syrup began to bubble, he smiled.

"Maybe that's what I can do!" he exclaimed. "I'll try making a new candy — for Katie and all the children — a candy that tells about Christmas. Thank You, Lord!"

His eyes brightened. *What flavor should it be?* he wondered to himself. Katie likes peppermint. He picked up a small bottle, carefully added three drops to the pot, smelled the minty aroma, and said, "Mmmm. This reminds me of the wise men's gift of spices to Jesus."

The shopkeeper continued, "I want this candy to be white," said the old man. "Because Jesus is the holy Son of God. And it should be hard — hard as a rock — because He is the Solid Rock, always there when I need Him."

The candymaker poured the thick golden syrup into a bowl to cool. As he looked around his shop, he wondered to himself, *How can this candy be different from ordinary candy sticks?*

G reasing his hands with butter, he took the sticky glob from the bowl and began stretching it. The more he pulled, the smoother and whiter it became. He felt discouraged, though. *I just can't think of anything new. Show me what to do, Lord,* he prayed.

H is gaze fell upon the Nativity set, and an idea flashed in his mind. Quickly he rolled the candy into the shape of a rope. Then he cut a long piece and curved one end around. He held up the finished stick and said, "What will Katie and the other children think?"

Just then the door bells jingled again and Katie's familiar voice interrupted his thoughts. "Hi, Grandpa! I'm here!" She skipped across the room, a bundle of energy.

The shopkeeper laid his candy stick on the table and bent down to kiss the little girl's rosy cheeks. "Katie! How's my favorite granddaughter?"

"I'm your ONLY granddaughter!" said the girl, giggling as she hugged him. "Oh, Grandpa, come over tonight and see our Christmas tree. I made some decorations and I..." She stopped abruptly when she spotted the candy.

Katie's eyes widened and she picked up the candy stick. "What are you making, Grandpa? It's a funny shape."

The chair creaked as the candymaker sat down to watch her. "What do you think it is?" He wrinkled his brows, waiting for her answer.

She turned the stick sideways and around. "I know! It's a cane—like the one you take on your walks," she said with a grin.

*T*he old man laughed heartily. "It does look like my cane when you

hold it that way!"

Katie pointed to the figures in the window. "Grandpa, that shepherd has

a cane, too."

"You're right," he said. "It's called a *staff*. Shepherds use it to comfort their

sheep, guide them on the right path, and keep them out of trouble." He handed

her a candy stick. "Go ahead and taste the candy. I hope you like it."

While Katie licked the sweet stick, he continued, "This staff reminds us of

Jesus, our Good Shepherd. A good shepherd doesn't run away from danger, and

he will do anything to save his sheep."

*T*he grandfather picked up another candy stick. *How can I explain everything?* he wondered. Turning the stick upside down, he looked thoughtfully at his granddaughter and asked, "**Now** what do you see?"

Katie's eyes sparkled. "It's a 'J.' Why did you make a 'J'?"

He smiled. "Because we celebrate Jesus' birthday at Christmas. This candy 'J' is my special Christmas gift for **you.**"

"Thank you, Grandpa!" Katie squealed with delight. "It tastes yummy! And it smells good, too." She paused and looked at the candy. "But...it looks kind of plain. Could you make it **pretty**?"

$\mathcal{L}$ooking at the candy stick, the old man agreed. "You're right, Katie. It does look plain." He went over to a shelf full of small jars. "I wanted to make it white because Jesus is pure and without sin, but I'll try adding some color. What color would **you** pick?"

"Red — I like red for Christmas," Katie said.

He took a jar from the shelf and reached in the drawer for a small paintbrush. "What does red make you think of?" he asked.

*T*he little girl watched her grandfather dip his brush into the food coloring. "Red makes me think of hearts...and love," she said.

"Ah, you're helping me, dear girl." His paintbrush wound a swirl of red around the white stick. When he finished the long stripe, he paused. "The Bible says, *'For God so loved the world that He gave...'* Oh Katie, never forget the first Christmas gift. Do you know what that gift was?"

"Was Baby Jesus the first Christmas gift?" she asked.

"Yes," he answered. "Jesus was God's gift of **love** to the whole world. Adding this red stripe will remind us of God's great love." He began painting a second line around the candy stick. Now he spoke in a softer voice, "Red also makes me think of the blood of Jesus shed for us on the cross."

"Is that why you're painting another red line, Grandpa?"

The candymaker explained, "I want these stripes to remind us that Jesus suffered and died for us."

"It makes me sad that Jesus died," Katie said quietly.

"It is sad, but it's the way Jesus showed how much he loves us. When you taste the sweet candy, think about the sweetness of Jesus' love. And remember, Jesus isn't dead. He is alive! He came out of the grave and He lives with us today."

Katie nodded and smiled. "Someday we'll live with Jesus in heaven — just like Grandma."

"Yes, we will — forever and ever and ever! Heaven is God's gift that never ends." The old man's eyes glistened as he handed her the finished candy cane. "Watch how you hold it— it's not quite dry."

The elderly shopkeeper leaned back in his chair. "Well, what do you think of it, Katie-girl?"

"I like it, Grandpa! Can you make some more — for all my friends?"

"We can work together! After I cut each stick, you can curve one end."

"Oh, goodie — this will be fun!" Katie jumped up and down excitedly.

*T*ears of joy filled the candymaker's eyes.
Silently he prayed, *Thank You, Lord, for hearing my
prayers. You gave me the idea for this special candy and You
sent my Katie to help me.*

He smiled at his granddaughter. "Katie Dear, you were part of God's answer to
my prayers today. I wanted to give you a special gift, but you gave something to me.
You helped me make a candy that tells the real meaning of Christmas."

"Oh, Grandpa, it was fun to help you!" She threw her arms around his neck and
hugged him tightly.

"Let's thank God for helping us," said the old man, putting his arm around her. They knelt together and prayed that his candy cane gift would be a reminder of God's perfect gift of love — Jesus — and that through it many would learn the true meaning of Christmas.

The snow fell quietly outside, covering the little store with a white blanket. Inside, the warmth of the old wood stove and the sweet smell of candy filled the workshop. The candymaker knew in his heart that he and Katie would always remember this day, but they never dreamed the sweet gift would become a part of Christmas tradition around the world. Today we call it the candy cane.

❧ The End ❧

Candy Cane Celebrations!

*S*it down together by candlelight with mugs of hot cocoa. Unwrap candy canes and use them as stirring sticks. Mmmmm! Share your memories of past Christmases.

*T*alk about the different ways your family can share God's Love. Plan a party for neighbor children, a caroling visit to a children's hospital or nursing home. Take candy canes and explain their meaning.

*C*ut out and paint a white "stick," a white "J," and a striped cane. Practice telling each other about the candy cane's meaning. Take turns finishing the sentence: "The candy cane reminds me of..."

Invite friends over for a "Candy Cane Party."
Here are some ideas:

❋ Ask guests to dress in red and white.

❋ Play Christmas charades (act out Christmas carols).

❋ Draw & guess parts of the Christmas story (manger, camel, angel).

❋ Read The Candymaker's Gift (while guests lick candy canes).

❋ Let children take turns explaining the candy cane.

❋ Prepare a batch of play dough — make candy cane ornaments.

❋ Bake bread, rolls, and cookies in "cane" shapes.

❋ Serve red & white snacks (like strawberry sundaes, muffins & jam, or sliced apples, bananas, and grapes).

*P*ray for those with whom you will share the meaning of Christmas and of the candy cane — neighbors, friends, schoolmates, relatives. Kneel together and thank God for the first Christmas gift — Jesus.

Decorate with a *Candy Cane* Theme

Decorate your Christmas tree with candy canes of various sizes. To hang them like a cane or staff, tie heavy gold thread in a loop around the curve of the candy canes. To hang them like a "J", glue gold thread to the bottom of each candy cane.

Front Yard Candy Stick

Decorate your mail box or yard light pole with strips of red plastic or oilcloth to make it look like stripes on a candy cane. Your giant "candy stick" can provide opportunities to share its meaning.

Candy Cane Flower Vase

Turn a plain jar or coffee can into a Christmas flowerpot. Place 2 rows of 2-3 heavy rubber bands around the upper and lower third of 7-8" tall can or jar. Slip 8" or 9" candy canes side by side under the rubber bands. (You need about 20-24 canes to go around a 4" diameter can.) Tie red or green ribbons around the can or jar to cover the rubber bands.

Candy Cane Cookies

1 1/2 cups powdered sugar
1 cup (2 sticks) butter, softened
1 teaspoon vanilla
1 egg

1/2 teaspoon salt
1 teaspoon baking soda
2-1/2 cups white flour
1 teaspoon red food coloring (add to half the batch)

Mix sugar, butter, vanilla, and egg in one bowl. Mix dry ingredients together, then add to sugar/butter mixture. Stir until the dough forms a ball.

Divide dough in half. Place half in another bowl, add red food coloring, and mix. You can also make two batches of cookie dough and color one batch red.)

Cover each ball of dough with wax paper. Refrigerate one hour.

Heat oven to 350 degrees. Using a tablespoon of dough, roll with hands and fingers into the shape and size of a pencil. Place one red and one white strand side by side and twist gently together. Curve one end like a cane. Bake on ungreased cookie sheet 8-11 minutes. Do not brown.

The Meaning of the Candy Cane

Hard Candy:
Reminds us that Jesus is like a "rock," strong and dependable.
(Read Psalm 31:3.)

Peppermint Flavor:
Is like the gift of spices from the wise men.
(Read Matthew 2:11.)

White Candy:
Stands for Jesus as the holy, sinless Son of God.
(Read 1 John 1:7.)

Cane:
Is like a staff used by shepherds in caring for sheep. Jesus is our "Good Shepherd."
(Read John 10:11-18.)

The Letter "J":
Is for the Name of Jesus, our Savior.
(Read Matthew 1:21.)

The Color Red:
Is for God's love that sent Jesus to give his life for us on the cross.
(Read John 3:16 and Revelation 1:5.)

The Stripes:
Remind us of Jesus' suffering — his crown of thorns,
the wounds in his hands and feet; and the cross on which he died.
(Read John 19:1-30.)

Receive God's Christmas Gift

The following verses are God's words of love from the
New International Version of the Bible:

God tells you how much you are loved: "For God so loved the world that he gave his one and only Son, that whoever (that's you!) believes in him shall not perish, but have eternal life." John 3:16

No one lives a perfect life. No one does everything that is right: "For all have sinned and fall short of the glory of God." Romans 3:23

Our wrongdoing separates us from God: "For the wages of sin is death; but the gift of God is eternal life in Christ Jesus our Lord." Romans 6:23

God sent Jesus to die for us and take our punishment: "God demonstrates his own love for us in this: While we were still sinners, Christ died for us." Romans 5:8

Jesus says to you, "Here I am! I stand at the door and knock. If anyone hears my voice and opens the door, I will come in and eat with him, and he with me." Revelation 3:20

Open the door of your heart to Jesus. Pray a prayer like this:
Thank You, Jesus, for dying on the cross for me. Please forgive all I've done wrong. Come into my life and be my Savior. Thank You for loving me and promising me a home in heaven. Help me live for You. Amen.

You can be sure of God's gift of eternal life:
"If you confess with your mouth, 'Jesus is Lord,' and believe in your heart that God raised him from the dead, you will be saved." Romans 10:9.